Northamptonshire County Council
Libraries and Information Service

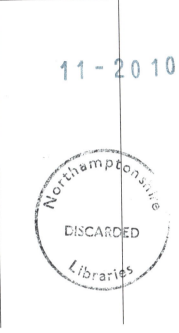

11 - 2010

WHYBROW, I.   F4

Fix it with bubble gum

Please return or renew this item by the last date shown.
You may renew items (unless they have been requested
by another customer) by telephoning, wr'
in at any library.   100% recycled paper

04412

80 001 576 492

for Rooby Dooby and Luce
I.W.
for Louise and Rosie

ORCHARD BOOKS
96 Leonard Street, London, EC2A 4RH
Orchard Books Australia
14 Mars Road, Lane Cove, NSW 2066
First published in Great Britain 1995
First paperback publication 1996
Text © Ian Whybrow 1995
Illustrations © Tim Archbold 1995
The right of Ian Whybrow to be identified as the Author
and Tim Archbold as the Illustrator
of this Work has been asserted by them
in accordance with the Copyright,
Designs and Patents Act, 1988.
A CIP catalogue record for this book is
available from the British Library.
1 85213 925 0 (hardback)
1 86039 095 1 (paperback)
Printed in Great Britain.

Ian Whybrow

Illustrated by Tim Archbold

ORCHARD BOOKS

This is Art.
This is the Shrinky Kid.

He hasn't got the measles.
He's got the shoebox.
There's something in the shoebox,
something good.
But the shoebox comes later.
After the measles.
We must start with the measles.

Forget the box for now.
It's just a shoebox.
Put the shoebox away, Art.
Art!

Put the shoebox under the bed.
Thank you.

Now get off the picture.
Not under the bed, thank you.

Go downstairs and get on the sofa.
Thank you.
Now we can start with the measles.

Art was not well.
Art had the measles.
The doctor said so.

The doctor said, "Hmmm. Yes.
Red eyes."

The doctor said, "Hmmm. Yes.
Spots behind the ears."

The doctor said, "Dear me, yes.
Cough and a fever!"
The doctor said,
"Bed for this boy!
This boy has got the measles!"

Art's mother said,
"May he lie on the sofa, doctor?"
The doctor said,
"Sofas are all very well
for tickly throats
but not for measles."

The doctor said,
"For the measles
BED is best."
The doctor said,
"Keep him warm.
Draw the curtains.
And give him plenty to drink."

"Oh goodie!" said Art's mother.
(She *loved* to keep fit.)
She put on her track suit.
She touched her toes.
She pumped up her muscles
and she carried Art up to bed.

She drew the curtains,
to rest Art's eyes.
Then she tiptoed downstairs
and waited.
In the kitchen she took her marks.
She got set.
Then it was READY...
STEADY...

For the next two days,
it was up and down for Art's
mother.

She ran
up with the milk

and down with the glass

and up with the juice

and down with the mug

and up with the tea

and down with the cup

and up with the tray

and down with the tray.

And she pulled up the quilt
that fell off the bed.
And poured down the medicine
for Art's sore head.

She tidied the room
and she emptied the potty.
And poor little Art
got more and more spotty.

And on the third day…
Art started to feel a bit better.
And that was when
Art started to feel a bit bored.
So his mum brought him Lego
but he didn't want Lego.

She brought him books
but he didn't want books.
And he didn't want jigsaws
and he didn't want Gameboys.
And he didn't want radio
or telly or tapes
or apples or pears
or bananas or grapes.

So his mum said,
"Puff puff – listen Art,
I *love* to keep fit
but I've been up and down
those stairs for three days!
Will you please make up
your mind!

IS THIS WHAT YOU WANT?

IS THIS WHAT YOU WANT?

IS THIS WHAT YOU WANT?"

Then she said,
"What do you want? Just make up
your mind!"

"Thanks, Mum," whispered Art.
"Have you got anything…different?"

Art's mum took
a deep breath.
She had a good
think.
At first she couldn't
think of anything.
Then she thought
of the attic.

"There's something in the attic,"
she said.

And she went up to the attic
and fetched Art the shoebox.

Art was difficult.
"What's this, a shoebox?" Art said.
"Who wants shoes?"
He pushed the shoebox away.
Art's mum said,
"These are not shoes.
These are what I made myself
when I was eight years old.
Take a look."

Moooo! Wuff-Wuff!

Art said, "I don't like surprises.
Not when I'm ill.
My head hurts."
Art's mum said,
"Guess what's inside.
Shall I give you a hint?
Baaaa!" she said.

Art was grumpy.
"I hate hints," he said.
"I hate shoeboxes."

Art's mother said, "OK, Art.
OK, Art. You just rest.
The shoebox can wait.
I'm going downstairs."

Cluck -Cluck!

Off she went
and the shoebox waited.
It waited and waited
at the end of the bed.
Art tried to ignore it.
But then he started wondering.
He wondered some more.
Then he crawled to the end of the
bed and lifted the lid.

Very gently, he tipped up the
shoebox and out fell
a red tractor,

an orange sheep
and two orange lambs,
a yellow pig,
a green horse,
a blue chicken,
an indigo cow,
a violet cat with a piano,
and a dotty dog with three legs.

The green horse got up.
"Hello," he said. "I'm Hoofer.
I can dance but I can't mend
things. Can you mend things?"
"Um, some things," Art said.
"What needs mending?"

"We can talk better if you shrink," said Hoofer.

"How do I do that?" said Art.

"Just thinky thanky thunky," said Hoofer.

So Art went thinky thanky thunky
till he shrinky shranky shrunky

and he was no bigger than the
violet cat's piano.

Art was surprised.
He was surprised to be shrunk.
He was surprised to be talking to a green horse.

"Do you all talk?" said Art.

"Yup," said Hoofer. "Everybody in
the shoebox. We can all talk.
Only we don't talk
with grown-ups around.
Violet the cat can play the piano.
But I'm the best dancer. Watch."

Violet the cat got up.
She walked on the keys to make the music.
Hoofer danced. He was the best!

"Wow, man!" said Violet.

Art said, "You know what?
You should be on TV."

"One day I will be," said Hoofer.

The tractor got up.
"Hi, I'm Red," said the tractor.
"Are you the mender?"

"Well, I can mend *some* things,"
said Art.
"What needs mending?"

"My wheel," said Red.
"I love to brrrm but when I get
excited my wheel falls off. Look."
He brrmmed up and down
very fast and his wheel fell off.
He started to cry.

"Oh dear," said Art, "I see what
you mean."

Chucky the blue chicken got up.
She was very bossy.
"Stop crying, Red!
Stop that crying!" said Chucky.
"Leave this to me! I'll mend your
wheel! I'll mend it with straw.
No peace for the chicken! Perk!"

Indigo the indigo cow got up.
"Now don't fuss, Chucky," she said.
"Let me mother him.
I'll mend your wheel, Red.
I'll put a bandage on it, shall I?"

Red cried even louder.

Peewee the yellow pig got up.
"How about a mud wheel?"
said Peewee.
"Let me make you a mud wheel. I
am an artist with mud. Unk unk."

Maa the orange sheep got up.
"Red doesn't want a mud wheel,"
she said.
"He wants Maaa Sheep to count
his lights.
Me and my lambs, One and
Two, we love to count."

"Waaa," said One.
"Taaa," said Two.
"Can we count your lights?
Ca-a-a-an we? Ca-a-a-an we?"

"I don't want to be counted,"
cried Red.
"I want the mender to mend
my wheel!"

"I would mend it," said Dots the
dog, "but I've only got three legs.
Huff-huff!"
He tried to scratch but
he fell over.

"Wait, I'll be the mender!" said Art.
"I'll mend your wheel, Red!
I'll mend your leg, Dots!"

He closed his eyes till he was
normal size. Then he jumped
out of bed and he found a nail
and some bubble gum.

He mended Red's wheel
with the nail.

He made a leg for Dots with the
bubble gum.

Then he went thinky thanky thunky

till he shrinky shranky shrunky.

Red and Dots were ever so excited.
Red brrrmed and brrrmed round
and round. He went very, very fast
but his wheel didn't come off, not
once.

"Thank you, Mender!" said Red.

"My name's Art," said Art.
"Thank you, Art," said Red.
"Jump on, I'll give you a ride!"

"Let's pull the roller," said Art.
He hooked it on behind Red
and jumped into the driver's seat.
Off they went, rolling and brrrm
brrrming.

"Look at me!" said Dots.
"Look at me scratching!"
And he scratched himself so hard
with his bubble gum leg
that coloured dots flew everywhere
and landed on all the animals.

"Now everybody's got the
measles!" said Art.

"Party!!" said Peewee.
"It must be mud time!
Let's make mud cakes to eat
and fizz-whizz to drink!"

Hoofer said, "Come on, Maaa.
Come on, One and Two -
You can count the cakes!"

"Maaa!" said One.
"Taaa!" said Two.
Indigo laid the table.

Everyone had a marvellous mucky
teatime.
Then there were footsteps
on the stairs.
"Perk! Somebody's coming!"
said Chucky Chicken.
"Quick! Quick! Into the shoebox!"

The door opened.
"You're quiet, Art, my spotty boy,"
said Art's mother.
"Are you OK?"

She saw the shoebox had its lid on.
"Have you finished with the
shoebox?" she said.
"Shall I put it away?"
"I haven't finished with it yet," said
Art.

"Oh," said Art's mother.
"But you said you hated it."
"That was before," said Art.
Art's mother said, "So when will
you finish with it?"

Answers to the Quiz

(upside down below)

1) Boots in toy box
2) Position of tennis ball
3) Writing in book
4) Time on clock
5) Position of car
6) Shoes under the bed